EASY SHALLOT COOKBOOK

50 DELICIOUS SHALLOT RECIPES; TECHNIQUES FOR COOKING WITH SHALLOTS

By
BookSumo Press
Copyright © by Saxonberg Associates
All rights reserved

Published by
BookSumo Press, a DBA of Saxonberg Associates
http://www.booksumo.com/

About the Author.

BookSumo Press is a publisher of unique, easy, and healthy cookbooks.

Our cookbooks span all topics and all subjects. If you want a deep dive into the possibilities of cooking with any type of ingredient. Then BookSumo Press is your go to place for robust yet simple and delicious cookbooks and recipes. Whether you are looking for great tasting pressure cooker recipes or authentic ethic and cultural food. BookSumo Press has a delicious and easy cookbook for you.

With simple ingredients, and even simpler step-by-step instructions BookSumo cookbooks get everyone in the kitchen chefing delicious meals.

BookSumo is an independent publisher of books operating in the beautiful Garden State (NJ) and our team of chefs and kitchen experts are here to teach, eat, and be merry!

INTRODUCTION

Welcome to *The Effortless Chef Series*! Thank you for taking the time to purchase this cookbook.

Come take a journey into the delights of easy cooking. The point of this cookbook and all BookSumo Press cookbooks is to exemplify the effortless nature of cooking simply.

In this book we focus on Shallot. You will find that even though the recipes are simple, the taste of the dishes are quite amazing.

So will you take an adventure in simple cooking? If the answer is yes please consult the table of contents to find the dishes you are most interested in.

Once you are ready, jump right in and start cooking.

— BookSumo Press

TABLE OF CONTENTS

About the Author 2

Introduction 3

Table of Contents 4

Any Issues? Contact Us 8

Legal Notes 9

Common Abbreviations 10

Chapter 1: Easy Shallot Recipes 11

    Brenda's Bruschetta 11

    4-Ingredient Spinach 14

    Asiago Mushroom Sauce 16

    Green Bean Dream 18

    Mushroom Beef Skillet 20

    Rocky Mountain Asparagus 23

    Spicy Dijon Green Beans 25

    Summer Honey Salad 28

    Skinny Girl Breen Bean Lunch 31

Real Buffalo Burgers 34
Southwestern Panini 37
American Mashed Dinner Potatoes 40
November's Apricot Turkey 43
Argentinian Grilled Meat Sauce 47
(Chimichurri) 47
Amelia Island Oysters 49
Athens Pasta Salad 52
French Steak Sauce 55
Seafood Wellington 57
Authentic Asian Marinade for Grilling 60
Long Island Sound Salad 62
5 Star Butter 64
Upscale Artichokes 66
Southern Carolina BBQ Sauce 68
Potluck Party Dip 70
Tuna Salad Lunch 73
City View Soup 76
Boca Chica Oysters 78
Saturday's Dinner Platter 80

Late October Potatoes 83
Thursday's Tenderloin 86
Veggie Stir Fry 89
Texas Fritters 92
Bangkok South Squid 95
Nanjing Dynasty Chicken 98
Wild Salad 101
Award Winning Stuffing 103
Omega-3 Patties 107
Lamb Burgers Classical 110
New England Crab Lunch 113
Pilaf Possibilities 116
Mediterranean Fish 118
Central American Pasta 121
Augusta Pudding 124
Avenida Salsa 127
Scallop Platter 129
Broccoli Soup 132
How to Stuffed Mushrooms 134
Anniversary Night Marsala 137

Mississippi Corn 140

How to Make Egg Salad 142

THANKS FOR READING! JOIN THE CLUB AND KEEP ON COOKING WITH 6 MORE COOKBOOKS.... 145

Come On.. 147

Let's Be Friends :).. 147

ANY ISSUES? CONTACT US

If you find that something important to you is missing from this book please contact us at info@booksumo.com.

We will take your concerns into consideration when the 2nd edition of this book is published. And we will keep you updated!

— BookSumo Press

Legal Notes

ALL RIGHTS RESERVED. NO PART OF THIS BOOK MAY BE REPRODUCED OR TRANSMITTED IN ANY FORM OR BY ANY MEANS. PHOTOCOPYING, POSTING ONLINE, AND / OR DIGITAL COPYING IS STRICTLY PROHIBITED UNLESS WRITTEN PERMISSION IS GRANTED BY THE BOOK'S PUBLISHING COMPANY. LIMITED USE OF THE BOOK'S TEXT IS PERMITTED FOR USE IN REVIEWS WRITTEN FOR THE PUBLIC.

COMMON ABBREVIATIONS

cup(s)	C.
tablespoon	tbsp
teaspoon	tsp
ounce	oz.
pound	lb

*All units used are standard American measurements

Chapter 1: Easy Shallot Recipes

Brenda's Bruschetta

Ingredients

- 12 roma tomatoes, chopped
- 1 tbsp minced garlic
- 2 tbsp minced shallots
- 1 C. chopped fresh basil leaves
- 1 tsp fresh lemon juice
- salt to taste
- freshly ground black pepper to taste
- 1/3 C. extra virgin olive oil
- 3 cloves garlic, cut into slivers
- 1/4 C. extra virgin olive oil
- 1 (1 lb.) loaf Italian bread, cut into 1/2 inch slices

Directions

- In a large bowl, add the roma tomatoes, minced garlic, shallots, basil, lemon juice, salt, pepper and 1/3 C. of the olive oil and toss to coat well.
- In a small pan, add the slivered garlic and 1/4 C. of the olive oil on medium heat and cook for about 2-3 minutes.

- With a slotted spoon, discard the garlic.
- Toast the bread slices and then coat with the garlic oil.
- Place the roma tomato mixture over the slices and serve.

Amount per serving (16 total)

Timing Information:

Preparation	
Cooking	15 m
Total Time	15 m

Nutritional Information:

Calories	162 kcal
Fat	9.2 g
Carbohydrates	16.7g
Protein	3.1 g
Cholesterol	0 mg
Sodium	168 mg

* Percent Daily Values are based on a 2,000 calorie diet.

4-Ingredient Spinach

Ingredients

- 1 tbsp olive oil
- 1 shallot, diced
- 1 (10 oz.) bag baby spinach leaves
- kosher salt and freshly ground pepper to taste

Directions

- In a large skillet, heat the olive oil on medium heat and sauté the shallots for about 5 minutes.
- Add the spinach, salt and pepper and cook for about 3-5 minutes.

Amount per serving (4 total)

Timing Information:

Preparation	5 m
Cooking	8 m
Total Time	13 m

Nutritional Information:

Calories	55 kcal
Fat	3.7 g
Carbohydrates	4.7g
Protein	2.3 g
Cholesterol	0 mg
Sodium	158 mg

* Percent Daily Values are based on a 2,000 calorie diet.

Asiago Mushroom Sauce

Ingredients

- 2 lobster mushrooms, cut into cubes
- 2 tbsp water
- 1/3 C. heavy whipping cream
- 2 tsp all-purpose flour
- 2 tbsp grated Asiago cheese
- 1/2 shallot, minced
- 1/2 tsp salt
- 1/2 tsp ground black pepper

Directions

- In a nonstick skillet, add the mushrooms and water on medium heat and cook for about 5 minutes, stirring occasionally.
- Add the cream and flour and beat till the flour is well combined.
- Add the Asiago cheese, shallot, salt and black pepper to mushroom mixture and cook for about 7 minutes, stirring continuously.

Amount per serving (3 total)

Timing Information:

Preparation	10 m
Cooking	15 m
Total Time	25 m

Nutritional Information:

Calories	123 kcal
Fat	11.1 g
Carbohydrates	4.1g
Protein	2.5 g
Cholesterol	40 mg
Sodium	454 mg

* Percent Daily Values are based on a 2,000 calorie diet.

GREEN BEAN DREAM

Ingredients

- 1 tbsp butter
- 3 tbsp olive oil
- 1 large shallot, chopped
- 8 cloves garlic, sliced
- 15 oz. fresh green beans, trimmed
- salt and ground black pepper to taste
- 1/2 C. grated Parmesan cheese

Directions

- In a large skillet, melt the butter and olive oil on medium heat and cook the shallot and garlic for about 5-10 minutes, stirring occasionally.
- Stir in the green beans, salt and pepper and cook for about 12 minutes.
- Remove from the heat and serve with a sprinkling of the Parmesan cheese.

Amount per serving (5 total)

Timing Information:

Preparation	10 m
Cooking	20 m
Total Time	30 m

Nutritional Information:

Calories	169 kcal
Fat	12.8 g
Carbohydrates	10g
Protein	5.3 g
Cholesterol	13 mg
Sodium	177 mg

* Percent Daily Values are based on a 2,000 calorie diet.

Mushroom Beef Skillet

Ingredients

- 1 (2 lb.) boneless beef chuck roast, cut into serving-sized pieces
- 1/2 tsp salt
- 1/4 tsp ground black pepper
- 1 tbsp olive oil
- 8 oz. small shallots, peeled
- 3 cloves garlic, minced
- 1 (8 oz.) package mushrooms, cut in quarters
- 2 tbsp all-purpose flour
- 1 (14.5 oz.) can diced tomatoes
- 1 C. Swanson(R) Beef Stock
- 3 tbsp balsamic vinegar
- 1 tbsp packed brown sugar
- 1 lemon
- 1/4 C. chopped fresh parsley

- Directions
- Sprinkle the beef with the salt and black pepper evenly.
- In a 12-inch skillet, heat the oil on medium-high heat and sear the beef till browned from all sides.
- Transfer the beef into a bowl and keep aside.

- Drain the grease, leaving 1 tbsp in the skillet.
- In the skillet, add the shallots and cook for about 10 minutes, stirring occasionally.
- Add the garlic, mushrooms and flour and cook for about 1 minute.
- Stir in the tomatoes.
- In a bowl, add the stock, vinegar and brown sugar and mix till smooth.
- Stir in the stock mixture and bring to a boil.
- Return the beef to the skillet.
- Reduce the heat to low and simmer for about 1 1/2 hours.
- Uncover the skillet and simmer for about 30 minutes.
- Grate 2 tbsp of the zest from the lemon.
- In a bowl, mix together the lemon zest and parsley.
- Serve the beef mixture with a sprinkling of the lemon zest.

Amount per serving (4 total)

Timing Information:

Preparation	
Cooking	35 m
Total Time	3 h

Nutritional Information:

Calories	486 kcal
Fat	27.8 g
Carbohydrates	27.1g
Protein	33 g
Cholesterol	103 mg
Sodium	656 mg

* Percent Daily Values are based on a 2,000 calorie diet.

Rocky Mountain Asparagus

Ingredients

- 2 bunches fresh asparagus spears, trimmed
- 4 medium shallots, thinly sliced
- 4 tbsp extra-virgin olive oil
- 3 tbsp red wine vinegar, divided
- salt and pepper to taste

Directions

- Set your oven to 400 degrees F before doing anything else.
- In a large bowl, add the asparagus, shallots, olive oil, 2 tbsp of the vinegar, salt and pepper and toss to coat evenly.
- In a baking sheet, place the asparagus spears in a single layer.
- Cook in the oven for about 20 minutes, shaking the pan once in the middle way.
- Remove from the oven.
- Drizzle with the remaining vinegar and gently, toss to coat.
- Serve immediately.

Amount per serving (4 total)

Timing Information:

Preparation	5 m
Cooking	20 m
Total Time	25 m

Nutritional Information:

Calories	206 kcal
Fat	13.8 g
Carbohydrates	18g
Protein	6.2 g
Cholesterol	0 mg
Sodium	11 mg

* Percent Daily Values are based on a 2,000 calorie diet.

Spicy Dijon Green Beans

Ingredients

- 1 slice turkey bacon
- 1/2 lb. thin French green beans
- 3 tbsp extra-virgin olive oil
- 2 tsp Dijon-style mustard
- 2 tsp white wine vinegar
- 1 tsp bacon drippings
- 1 tbsp minced shallot

Directions

- Heat a large skillet on medium-high heat and cook the bacon for about 10 minutes, turning occasionally.
- Transfer the bacon onto a paper towel lined plate to drain and then crumble it.
- Drain the excess grease from the skillet, reserving 1 tsp inside.
- Arrange a steamer basket into a pan and fill with water to just below the bottom of the steamer basket.
- Bring the water to a boil over high heat and steam the green beans, covered for about 3 minutes.
- Drain well and transfer into a bowl with bacon.

- In a bowl, add the olive oil, Dijon-style mustard, vinegar, bacon drippings and shallot and beat till well combined.
- Add the dressing over hot green beans and toss to coat well.
- Serve immediately.

Amount per serving (4 total)

Timing Information:

Preparation	20 m
Cooking	10 m
Total Time	30 m

Nutritional Information:

Calories	130 kcal
Fat	12.4 g
Carbohydrates	2.7g
Protein	1.5 g
Cholesterol	4 mg
Sodium	300 mg

* Percent Daily Values are based on a 2,000 calorie diet.

Summer Honey Salad

Ingredients

- 1/4 C. lemon juice
- 2 tbsp honey
- 1 tbsp minced shallot
- 1 tsp chopped fresh thyme
- 1/2 tsp salt
- 1/4 tsp red pepper flakes
- 2 tbsp olive oil
- 2 tbsp vegetable oil
- 1 C. slivered almonds
- 2 tbsp white sugar
- 1 pinch salt
- 1 (16 oz.) package mixed salad greens
- 1/2 pint strawberries, quartered

Directions

- In a bowl, mix together the lemon juice, honey, shallot, thyme, salt and red pepper flakes.
- Add the olive oil, vegetable oil and lemon juice and beat till well combined.

- Heat a small skillet on medium-high heat and cook the almonds, sugar and salt for about 2-3 minutes, stirring continuously.
- Immediately, remove from the heat and keep aside.
- In a large bowl, place the salad mix.
- Pour the dressing over the salad and toss to coat.
- Serve with a toping of the caramelized almonds and strawberries.

Amount per serving (4 total)

Timing Information:

Preparation	15 m
Cooking	2 m
Total Time	17 m

Nutritional Information:

Calories	371 kcal
Fat	27.7 g
Carbohydrates	28.9g
Protein	8 g
Cholesterol	0 mg
Sodium	321 mg

* Percent Daily Values are based on a 2,000 calorie diet.

Skinny Girl Breen Bean Lunch

Ingredients

- 1/4 C. blanched slivered almonds
- 3 tbsp butter
- 5 small shallots, thinly sliced
- 1 red bell pepper, chopped
- 2 tbsp white sugar
- salt and pepper to taste
- 1 1/2 lb. fresh green beans, trimmed and snapped

Directions

- Heat a small dry skillet on low heat and cook the slivered almonds or about 3-5 minutes, stirring continuously.
- Immediately, remove from the heat and keep aside.
- In a skillet, melt the butter on medium-low heat and cook the shallots and red bell pepper for about 8 minutes.
- Sprinkle with the sugar, salt and pepper, and reduce heat to low.
- Cook, covered for about 5-8 minutes, stirring occasionally.
- Arrange a steamer basket into a pan and fill with water to just below the bottom of the steamer basket.

- Bring the water to a boil over high heat and steam the green beans for about 7-8 minutes.
- Drain the green beans and transfer into the skillet with the shallot mixture.
- Add the toasted almonds and gently stir to combine.

Amount per serving (6 total)

Timing Information:

Preparation	20 m
Cooking	25 m
Total Time	45 m

Nutritional Information:

Calories	148 kcal
Fat	8.3 g
Carbohydrates	17.1g
Protein	3.7 g
Cholesterol	15 mg
Sodium	51 mg

* Percent Daily Values are based on a 2,000 calorie diet.

Real Buffalo Burgers

Ingredients

- 1 C. pomegranate juice
- 1/2 C. chopped dried figs, stems removed
- 2 tbsp butter
- 1/2 C. thinly sliced shallots
- 1 tsp honey
- 1 tbsp chopped fresh thyme
- 1 egg, lightly beaten
- 2 lb. ground bison
- 1/4 C. soft bread crumbs
- 2 tbsp Worcestershire sauce
- 2 tbsp milk
- 2 cloves garlic, minced
- 1/2 tsp salt
- 1/4 tsp freshly ground black pepper
- 4 slices Gruyere cheese
- 4 slices toasted French bread

Directions

- In a small pan, add the pomegranate juice and bring to a boil on medium-high heat.

- Stir in the figs and remove from the heat.
- Keep aside for about 15 minutes, then drain the figs.
- For filling in a large skillet, melt the butter on medium-high heat and sauté the shallots for about 3-5 minutes.
- Add the drained figs and honey and stir to combine.
- Reduce the heat to low and cook for about 6-8, stirring occasionally.
- Stir in the thyme and remove from the heat.
- Keep aside to cool slightly.
- In a large bowl, add the egg, ground bison, bread crumbs, Worcestershire sauce, milk, garlic, salt and pepper and mix till well combined.
- Make 8 equal sized patties from the mixture.
- Place the filling over 4 patties evenly, to 1/2-inch of edges.
- Top with remaining patties and pinch the edges to seal.
- Place a drip pan over charcoal grill rack and arrange the preheated coals around the pan.
- Test for medium heat above the pan.
- Place bison patties over drip pan and cook, covered for about 16-22 minutes, flipping once in the middle way.
- Place 1 cheese over each patty and cook for about 1-2 minutes.
- Place the bison patties onto the French bread slices, open face side up.

Amount per serving (4 total)

Timing Information:

Preparation	30 m
Cooking	27 m
Total Time	1 h 12 m

Nutritional Information:

Calories	615 kcal
Fat	20.7 g
Carbohydrates	51.4g
Protein	55.6 g
Cholesterol	210 mg
Sodium	823 mg

* Percent Daily Values are based on a 2,000 calorie diet.

Southwestern Panini

Ingredients

- 3 tbsp unsalted butter
- 6 large shallots, sliced
- salt and black pepper to taste
- 2 French baguettes, halved lengthwise
- 2 tbsp Dijon mustard
- 1 C. Roquefort cheese, crumbled
- 1 lb. thinly sliced deli roast beef
- 1/2 C. cold heavy cream
- 1 1/2 tbsp finely shredded horseradish root
- 1 pinch salt and white pepper to taste

Directions

- In a large pan, melt the butter on medium heat and cook the shallots for about 10 minutes.
- Stir in the salt and black pepper and remove from the heat.
- Set your panini press according to manufacturer's
- Directions.
- Spread the Dijon mustard over the cut sides of the baguettes and sprinkle with the Roquefort cheese evenly.

- Place the roast beef over the bottom pieces of the baguettes and top with the shallots.
- Cover with the top pieces and cut each sandwich into 2-3 pieces.
- Cook the sandwiches onto the preheated Panini press for about 4 minutes.
- Meanwhile in a metal bowl, add the heavy cream and beat till the soft peaks form.
- Stir in the horseradish, salt and white pepper.
- Cut each sandwich in half and serve alongside the horseradish cream.

Amount per serving (6 total)

Timing Information:

Preparation	10 m
Cooking	15 m
Total Time	25 m

Nutritional Information:

Calories	652 kcal
Fat	23.3 g
Carbohydrates	77.3g
Protein	34.7 g
Cholesterol	96 mg
Sodium	1983 mg

* Percent Daily Values are based on a 2,000 calorie diet.

American Mashed Dinner Potatoes

Ingredients

- 6 tbsp minced shallots
- 2 tsp olive oil
- 1/2 C. low fat, low chicken broth
- 2 tsp minced fresh thyme
- ground black pepper to taste
- salt to taste
- 3 small Yukon Gold potatoes
- 1/2 C. evaporated skim milk

Directions

- Set your oven to 400 degrees F before doing anything else.
- In a small casserole dish, mix together the shallots, oil, broth, thyme, pepper and salt.
- Cover the casserole dish and cook in the oven for about 45 minutes.
- Remove the casserole dish from the oven.
- In a large pot of boiling water, cook the potatoes for about 20 minutes.
- Drain well and return the potatoes in the pan on low heat to dry.

- In a small pan, heat the milk on medium-low heat.
- Add the milk into the potatoes and with a mixer, beat till well combined.
- Add the roasted shallots and beat till the mixture becomes smooth.

Amount per serving (6 total)

Timing Information:

Preparation	10 m
Cooking	40 m
Total Time	1 h 30 m

Nutritional Information:

Calories	76 kcal
Fat	1.7 g
Carbohydrates	12.5g
Protein	3 g
Cholesterol	< 1 mg
Sodium	61 mg

* Percent Daily Values are based on a 2,000 calorie diet.

November's Apricot Turkey

Ingredients

- 1 C. apricot nectar
- 1 C. apricot preserves
- 2 tbsp minced fresh ginger root
- 1 tbsp honey
- 3/4 C. unsalted butter, softened
- 3 tbsp chopped fresh sage
- 1 1/2 tsp salt
- 1 tsp ground black pepper
- 2 tbsp unsalted butter
- 3 onions, thinly sliced
- 6 oz. thinly sliced shallots
- 22 lb. whole turkey
- 1 (14.5 oz.) can chicken broth
- 1 tsp chopped fresh thyme
- 1 tsp dried sage
- 1 (14.5 oz.) can chicken broth
- salt and pepper to taste

Directions

- For the glaze in a heavy small pan, add the apricot nectar, preserves, ginger and honey and bring to a boil.
- Reduce the heat to medium-low and simmer for about 15 minutes or till the mixture reduces to 1-1/4 C.

- For the herb butter in a small bowl, add 3/4 C. of the softened unsalted butter, 3 tbsp of the chopped fresh sage, salt and pepper mix till well combined.
- For the onion mixture in a heavy large skillet, melt 2 tbsp of the unsalted butter on medium heat and cook the onions and shallots for about 20 minutes.
- Set your oven to 400 degrees F and arrange a rack in lowest third of the oven.
- Arrange a rack in a large roasting pan.
- With the paper towels, pat dry the turkey.
- Rub thee turkey cavity with the salt and pepper evenly.
- Place the turkey over the rack in roasting pan.
- With your fingers, loosen the skin of turkey breast.
- Spread half of the herb butter under the skin of turkey breast.
- In a small pan, add the remaining herb butter on low heat and cook till melted completely.
- Coat the outside of the turkey with the melted butter evenly.
- With the kitchen strings loosely, tie the legs together to hold the shape of turkey.
- Cook in the oven for about 30 minutes.
- Now, set your oven to 325 degrees F and cook for about 1 hour 30 minutes, coating with the pan drippings occasionally.
- Now, with a piece of the foil, cover the turkey and cook for about 45 minutes.

- In the roasting pan, add the onion mixture, 1 can of the broth, thyme and 1/2 tsp of the chopped fresh sage and cook for about 15 minutes.
- Uncover the turkey and coat with 1/2 C. of the hot glaze and cook for about 40 minutes, coating with the hot glaze occasionally.
- Remove from the oven and place the turkey onto platter.
- With a piece of the foil, cover the turkey for about 30 minutes.
- For gravy through a strainer, strain the roasting pan contents into a large bowl.
- With a slotted spoon, remove the fat from the pan juices.
- In a blender, add the onion mixture and 1 C. of the pan juices and pulse till smooth, adding more pan juices and chicken broth if required.
- In a large pan, add the pureed mixture and bring to boil.
- Cook for about 5 minutes, skimming off any foam from the top surface.
- Stir in the salt and pepper and remove from the heat.
- Serve the turkey with the gravy.

Amount per serving (22 total)

Timing Information:

Preparation	30 m
Cooking	2 h 20 m
Total Time	3 h

Nutritional Information:

Calories	808 kcal
Fat	39.4 g
Carbohydrates	14.8g
Protein	93.2 g
Cholesterol	287 mg
Sodium	507 mg

* Percent Daily Values are based on a 2,000 calorie diet.

Argentinian Grilled Meat Sauce (Chimichurri)

Ingredients

- 1/2 C. olive oil
- 2 tbsp fresh lemon juice
- 1 tsp minced garlic
- 1/3 C. minced shallot
- 1/3 C. minced fresh parsley
- 1 tsp chopped fresh basil
- 1 tsp chopped fresh thyme
- 1 tsp chopped fresh oregano
- Salt and ground black pepper to taste

Directions

- In a bowl, add the olive oil, lemon juice, garlic, shallot, parsley, basil, thyme, oregano, salt and pepper and mix till well combined.
- Keep in the room temperature for about 2 hours before serving.
- You can store the remaining chimichurri in refrigerator.

Amount per serving (8 total)

Timing Information:

Preparation	
Cooking	15 m
Total Time	2 h 15 m

Nutritional Information:

Calories	127 kcal
Fat	13.5 g
Carbohydrates	1.8g
Protein	0.3 g
Cholesterol	0 mg
Sodium	3 mg

* Percent Daily Values are based on a 2,000 calorie diet.

Amelia Island Oysters

Ingredients

- 1 C. butter, softened
- 2 tbsp chopped fresh cilantro
- 3 tbsp minced garlic
- 2 tbsp minced shallot
- 2 tbsp lime juice
- 3 tbsp chili-garlic sauce (such as Sriracha(R))
- 12 fresh oysters in shells
- 2 tbsp lime juice

Directions

- In a medium bowl, add the butter, cilantro, garlic, shallot, 2 tbsp of the lime juice and sriracha sauce and mix till well combined.
- Place the mixture onto a waxed paper.
- Carefully, roll the waxed paper into a log and freeze till set.
- Set your grill for high heat and lightly, grease the grill grate.
- Cook the whole oysters onto the grill for about 3-5 minutes.

- Carefully, remove the top shell from the oysters, without spilling any liqueur.
- Return the oyster onto the grill.
- Cut the butter log into 1/4-inch slices.
- Arrange 1 butter slice on top of each oyster and cook onto the grill till the butter is melted.
- Serve the grilled oysters over a bed of rock salt for nice presentation.

Amount per serving (6 total)

Timing Information:

Preparation	30 m
Cooking	20 m
Total Time	50 m

Nutritional Information:

Calories	304 kcal
Fat	31 g
Carbohydrates	4.2g
Protein	3.7 g
Cholesterol	89 mg
Sodium	550 mg

* Percent Daily Values are based on a 2,000 calorie diet.

ATHENS PASTA SALAD

Ingredients

- 8 oz. whole wheat penne pasta
- 2 tbsp extra virgin olive oil
- 1 tbsp butter
- 1 (1 lb.) beef rib eye steak
- 1 tbsp butter
- 1 tsp minced garlic
- 1/4 C. chopped shallots
- 1 tbsp soy sauce
- 1/2 C. sun-dried tomato pesto
- 1/2 C. sliced black olives
- 1 C. chopped fresh spinach
- 1 tsp basil
- 1 tbsp chopped parsley
- 1/2 C. crumbled feta cheese
- 3 tbsp sunflower kernels

Directions

- In a large pan of lightly salted boiling water, cook the pasta for about 8-10 minutes.
- Drain well and transfer into a large bowl.

- Add the olive oil and toss to coat well.
- Keep aside the bowl, covered to keep the pasta warm.
- Meanwhile in a skillet, melt 1 tbsp of the butter on medium-high heat and sear the rib-eye from both sides for about 7-10 minutes.
- Transfer the steak onto a cutting board and cut into bite-size pieces.
- In the same skillet, melt the remaining 1 tbsp of the butter and sauté the garlic and shallots for about 5-10 seconds.
- Add the steak pieces and cook for about 5 minutes.
- Stir in the soy sauce and cook till it evaporate, stirring continuously.
- Remove from the heat and stir in the sun-dried tomato pesto, olives, spinach, basil, parsley, feta cheese and sunflower kernels.
- Add the beef mixture into the bowl with the pasta and toss to coat well.
- Serve immediately.

Amount per serving (4 total)

Timing Information:

Preparation	15 m
Cooking	20 m
Total Time	35 m

Nutritional Information:

Calories	579 kcal
Fat	35 g
Carbohydrates	44.7g
Protein	24.5 g
Cholesterol	73 mg
Sodium	710 mg

* Percent Daily Values are based on a 2,000 calorie diet.

French Steak Sauce

Ingredients

- 2 tbsp butter
- 1/4 C. finely minced shallots
- 6 tbsp finely chopped fresh parsley
- 1 tbsp crushed black pepper
- 1/2 tsp salt
- 1 C. cognac
- 1 1/2 C. beef stock
- 6 tbsp crème fraiche
- 2 tbsp butter

Directions

- In a pan, melt 2 tbsp of the butter on low heat and sauté the shallots for about 5 minutes.
- Stir in the parsley and sauté for about 5 minutes.
- Stir in the salt and pepper.
- Carefully pour the cognac over the shallot mixture and cook for about 2-3 minutes, stirring continuously.
- Add the beef stock and bring to a boil.
- Reduce the heat and stir in the crème fraiche.
- Simmer for about 5 minutes, stirring continuously.
- Add 2 tbsp of the butter into sauce and stir till melted.

Amount per serving (6 total)

Timing Information:

Preparation	10 m
Cooking	20 m
Total Time	30 m

Nutritional Information:

Calories	249 kcal
Fat	13.6 g
Carbohydrates	3.4g
Protein	2 g
Cholesterol	41 mg
Sodium	279 mg

* Percent Daily Values are based on a 2,000 calorie diet.

Seafood Wellington

Ingredients

- 2 tbsp olive oil
- 4 C. fresh spinach leaves
- salt and pepper to taste
- 1 sheet frozen puff pastry, thawed
- 4 jumbo shrimp, peeled and deveined
- 4 oz. crabmeat, drained and flaked
- 1/4 C. béchamel sauce
- 1 tbsp chopped shallots
- 1 tbsp chopped fresh tarragon
- 1 egg, beaten

Directions

- Set your oven to 400 degrees F before doing anything else and grease a baking sheet.
- In a large skillet, heat the oil on medium heat and cook the spinach for about 3 minutes.
- Stir in the salt and pepper and remove from the heat.
- Drain off any excess liquid from the skillet and keep aside.
- Place the puff pastry sheet onto a smooth surface and cut into 4 equal sized squares.
- With a fork, prick the squares lightly.

- In a bowl, add the crab meat, béchamel sauce, shallots and tarragon and mix till well combined.
- Cut the shrimp lengthwise and carefully, open each one o form a butterfly shape.
- In the center of each pastry square, place 1 shrimp, open side facing up.
- Stuff each shrimp with the spinach and top with the crab mixture evenly.
- Fold the pastry over the shrimp to make a triangle and press the edges to seal tightly.
- Arrange the pastries onto the prepared baking sheet in a single layer and coat with the beaten egg.
- Cook in the oven for about 15-20 minutes.
- Remove from the oven and keep aside to cool.
- These pastries are best when served warm.

Amount per serving (4 total)

Timing Information:

Preparation	15 m
Cooking	20 m
Total Time	35 m

Nutritional Information:

Calories	502 kcal
Fat	33.5 g
Carbohydrates	30g
Protein	20.1 g
Cholesterol	129 mg
Sodium	482 mg

* Percent Daily Values are based on a 2,000 calorie diet.

Authentic Asian Marinade for Grilling

Ingredients

- 1/3 C. soy sauce
- 1/4 C. rice vinegar
- 2 tbsp honey
- 2 tbsp sesame oil
- 2 tsp minced garlic
- 1 tbsp grated fresh ginger root
- 1 tbsp chopped green onion or shallot
- 1 tbsp raw sesame seeds
- 1/2 tsp ground pepper

Directions

- In a bowl, add all the ingredients and beat till the honey dissolves completely.

Amount per serving (6 total)

Timing Information:

Preparation	15 m
Cooking	30 m
Total Time	45 m

Nutritional Information:

Calories	80 kcal
Fat	5.3 g
Carbohydrates	7.9g
Protein	1.3 g
Cholesterol	0 mg
Sodium	803 mg

* Percent Daily Values are based on a 2,000 calorie diet.

Long Island Sound Salad

Ingredients

- 2 tbsp sour cream
- 2 tbsp mayonnaise
- 2 tbsp sweet pickle relish
- 1 large shallot, minced
- 1 1/2 tsp Worcestershire sauce
- 3/4 tsp dried dill weed
- 1/2 tsp chopped fresh parsley
- 1/4 tsp cayenne pepper
- 1/4 tsp paprika
- 1/4 tsp fresh lemon juice
- 1/4 tsp grated lemon zest
- freshly ground black pepper to taste
- 1 lb. crabmeat - drained, flaked and cartilage removed

Directions

- In a large bowl, add all the ingredients except the crab meat and mix till well combined.
- Add the crab meat and stir till combined well.
- Refrigerate, covered for at least 1 hour before serving.

Amount per serving (8 total)

Timing Information:

Preparation	
Cooking	12 m
Total Time	1 h 12 m

Nutritional Information:

Calories	100 kcal
Fat	4.2 g
Carbohydrates	3.1g
Protein	12 g
Cholesterol	53 mg
Sodium	252 mg

* Percent Daily Values are based on a 2,000 calorie diet.

5 Star Butter

Ingredients

- 1/2 C. unsalted butter
- 1 1/2 tsp lemon juice
- 1 tbsp dried tarragon
- 1 tsp freshly ground black pepper
- 2 tbsp minced shallots
- salt to taste

Directions

- In a small bowl, add the butter and with an electric mixer, beat till creamy.
- Add the lemon juice, tarragon, black pepper, shallot and salt and stir to combine.
- Refrigerate for at least 1 hour before serving.

Amount per serving (8 total)

Timing Information:

Preparation	5 m
Cooking	1 h
Total Time	1 h 5 m

Nutritional Information:

Calories	107 kcal
Fat	11.6 g
Carbohydrates	1g
Protein	0.4 g
Cholesterol	31 mg
Sodium	2 mg

* Percent Daily Values are based on a 2,000 calorie diet.

UPSCALE ARTICHOKES

Ingredients

- 2 artichokes, halved and choke scraped out
- 1 tsp salt
- 1 tsp ground black pepper
- 2 cloves garlic, chopped
- 1 shallot, chopped
- 1/2 C. butter

Directions

- Set your outdoor grill for low heat and lightly, grease the grill grate.
- In a large pan of the boiling water, cook the artichokes, salt, pepper, 1/2 of the garlic and 1/2 of the shallot for about 30 minutes.
- Drain well and keep aside.
- In a small pan, melt the butter on medium heat and sauté the remaining garlic and shallot till just fragrant.
- Immediately, remove from the heat.
- Coat the artichoke halves with some of the melted butter and cook onto the grill for about 5-10 minutes, coating with the butter occasionally.
- Serve the grilled artichokes alongside the remaining butter as a dipping sauce.

Amount per serving (4 total)

Timing Information:

Preparation	10 m
Cooking	50 m
Total Time	1 h 20 m

Nutritional Information:

Calories	254 kcal
Fat	23.2 g
Carbohydrates	11.5g
Protein	3.4 g
Cholesterol	61 mg
Sodium	823 mg

* Percent Daily Values are based on a 2,000 calorie diet.

SOUTHERN CAROLINA BBQ SAUCE

Ingredients

- 2 cloves garlic, minced
- 1 tbsp minced shallot
- 1/2 C. honey
- 2 C. barbecue sauce, your choice
- 3 tbsp chopped fresh cilantro

Directions

- In a medium, nonporous bowl, add all the ingredients and mix till well combined.
- Spread this sauce over the meat of your choice.
- Discard any remaining sauce.

Amount per serving (16 total)

Timing Information:

Preparation	
Cooking	15 m
Total Time	15 m

Nutritional Information:

Calories	80 kcal
Fat	0.1 g
Carbohydrates	20.3g
Protein	0.1 g
Cholesterol	0 mg
Sodium	350 mg

* Percent Daily Values are based on a 2,000 calorie diet.

Potluck Party Dip

Ingredients

- 1 C. unsalted butter
- 3/4 lb. feta cheese, crumbled
- 1 (8 oz.) package cream cheese, softened
- 2 cloves garlic, minced
- 1 shallot, minced
- 3 tbsp dry vermouth, optional
- ground white pepper, to taste
- 1/2 C. pine nuts, toasted
- 1 C. chopped sun-dried tomatoes
- 3/4 C. pesto sauce

Directions

- In a food processor, add the butter, feta cheese, cream cheese, garlic, shallot, vermouth and white pepper and pulse till smooth.
- Grease a gelatin mold and line with a plastic wrap.
- In the prepared gelatin mold, place a layer the dip, followed by the sun-dried tomatoes, pine nuts, pesto and cheese mixture.
- Repeat the layers.
- With the back of a spoon, pat down the layer slightly.

- Refrigerate for at least 1 hour.
- Carefully, invert the dip onto a serving plate and remove the plastic wrap.
- Serve this dip with the crackers of your choice.

Amount per serving (30 total)

Timing Information:

Preparation	
Cooking	20 m
Total Time	1 h 20 m

Nutritional Information:

Calories	162 kcal
Fat	15.2 g
Carbohydrates	2.9g
Protein	4.2 g
Cholesterol	36 mg
Sodium	234 mg

* Percent Daily Values are based on a 2,000 calorie diet.

Tuna Salad Lunch

Ingredients

- 1/2 C. mayonnaise
- 1 tbsp prepared Dijon-style mustard
- 1/4 tsp curry powder
- salt and pepper to taste
- 1 (6 oz.) can oil-packed tuna
- 1 shallot, finely chopped
- 1 Granny Smith apple, cored and diced
- 1/4 C. chopped walnuts
- 1/2 C. diced celery
- 1 tsp sweet pickle relish
- 4 large croissants
- 4 leaves lettuce
- 4 slices Swiss cheese

Directions

- In a bowl, add the mayonnaise, mustard, curry powder, salt and pepper and beat till well combined.
- Add the tuna, shallot, apple, walnuts, celery and pickle relish and toss to combine well.
- Lightly toast the croissants and then split in half.

- Arrange a lettuce leaf over the bottom half of each croissant and top with tuna salad evenly, followed by a Swiss cheese slice.
- Cover with the top half of the croissants.
- Serve alongside the dill pickle and potato chips.

Amount per serving (4 total)

Timing Information:

Preparation	15 m
Cooking	5 m
Total Time	20 m

Nutritional Information:

Calories	737 kcal
Fat	52 g
Carbohydrates	42.4g
Protein	26.2 g
Cholesterol	94 mg
Sodium	994 mg

* Percent Daily Values are based on a 2,000 calorie diet.

City View Soup

Ingredients

- 1/4 C. butter
- 1 C. chopped shiitake mushrooms
- 1 C. chopped Portobello mushrooms
- 2 shallots, chopped
- 2 tbsp all-purpose flour
- 1 (14.5 oz.) can chicken broth
- 1 C. half-and-half
- salt and pepper to taste
- 1 pinch ground cinnamon (optional)

Directions

- In a large pan, melt the butter on medium-high heat and sauté the mushrooms and shallots for about 5 minutes.
- Add the flour and cook till smooth, stirring continuously.
- Slowly, add the chicken broth and cook for about 5 minutes, stirring continuously.
- Stir in the half-and-half, salt, pepper and cinnamon and cook till heat completely.

Amount per serving (4 total)

Timing Information:

Preparation	10 m
Cooking	15 m
Total Time	25 m

Nutritional Information:

Calories	234 kcal
Fat	18.6 g
Carbohydrates	13.3g
Protein	4.4 g
Cholesterol	53 mg
Sodium	119 mg

* Percent Daily Values are based on a 2,000 calorie diet.

BOCA CHICA OYSTERS

Ingredients

- 1 tsp fennel seed, ground
- 1 C. butter, softened
- 1 tbsp shallots, minced
- 1 tbsp chopped fennel greens
- 1 tsp ground black pepper
- 1/2 tsp salt
- 24 unopened, fresh, live medium oysters

Directions

- Set your oven to 500 degrees F before doing anything else.
- In a small bowl, add the butter, ground fennel seeds, shallots, fennel bulb, fennel greens, pepper and salt and mix till well combined.
- Arrange the oysters over the oven rack and cook and cook in the oven for about 3-5 minutes.
- With an oyster knife, pry each oyster open at the hinge, loosen the oyster and discard the flat shell.
- Place about 1/2 tsp of the fennel butter over each oyster with and cook in the oven till the butter melts completely.

Amount per serving (24 total)

Timing Information:

Preparation	10 m
Cooking	30 m
Total Time	1 h 20 m

Nutritional Information:

Calories	77 kcal
Fat	7.8 g
Carbohydrates	0.5g
Protein	1.6 g
Cholesterol	24 mg
Sodium	110 mg

* Percent Daily Values are based on a 2,000 calorie diet.

Saturday's Dinner Platter

Ingredients

- 1 (.5 oz.) package dried forest mushroom blend
- 1 (.5 oz.) package dried shiitake mushrooms
- 2 tbsp olive oil
- 1 pheasant - deboned, skinned and cut into small chunks
- 1 1/2 tsp minced garlic
- 1 tsp dried basil
- 2 tbsp butter
- 1/4 C. finely chopped shallots
- 1 Portobello mushroom cap, chopped
- 3 tbsp sliced oil-packed sun-dried tomatoes
- 2 tbsp arrowroot powder
- salt to taste

Directions

- In a bowl of water, soak the dried mushrooms according to package's
- Drain and reserve the water.
- Cut the mushrooms into small pieces.
- In a large heavy skillet, heat the olive oil on medium heat and sauté the pheasant meat, garlic and basil till golden brown.

- With a slotted spoon, transfer the meat mixture into a plate and keep aside.
- In the same skillet, melt the butter to oil in skillet and sauté the shallots and chopped mushrooms till golden brown.
- Meanwhile in a small bowl, add 1/4 C. of the reserved mushroom soaking water and arrowroot powder and stir to combine.
- In the skillet, add the sun-dried tomatoes and the remaining mushroom soaking water and stir to combine.
- Add the arrowroot mixture into the mushroom mixture and stir to combine.
- Stir in the pheasant meat and simmer for about 30 minutes, stirring occasionally.

Amount per serving (4 total)

Timing Information:

Preparation	30 m
Cooking	1 h
Total Time	1 h 30 m

Nutritional Information:

Calories	538 kcal
Fat	31.9 g
Carbohydrates	12.5g
Protein	48 g
Cholesterol	157 mg
Sodium	720 mg

* Percent Daily Values are based on a 2,000 calorie diet.

Late October Potatoes

Ingredients

- 5 lb. sweet potatoes
- 1/2 C. unsalted butter, softened
- 1/2 tsp ground cardamom
- salt and pepper to taste
- 1 quart vegetable oil for frying
- 3/4 lb. thinly sliced shallots

Directions

- Set your oven to 400 degrees F before doing anything else.
- With a fork, prick each sweet potato and cook in the oven for about 1 hour.
- Now, set your oven to 250 degrees F.
- With a spoon, scoop the flesh from the skins of sweet potatoes and transfer into a bowl.
- Slowly, add the butter and cardamom, beating continuously till the mixture becomes smooth and fluffy.
- Stir in the salt and white pepper and transfer into a baking dish.
- Place the baking dish in the oven to keep warm.

- In a large deep skillet, heat 1-inch of oil and fry 1/2 of the shallots till crisp.
- With a slotted spoon, transfer the shallots onto a paper towel lined plate and sprinkle with the salt.
- Repeat with the remaining shallots.
- Serve the warm sweet potato mixture with a topping of the shallots.

Amount per serving (8 total)

Timing Information:

Preparation	10 m
Cooking	40 m
Total Time	1 h 20 m

Nutritional Information:

Calories	474 kcal
Fat	22.7 g
Carbohydrates	64.3g
Protein	5.7 g
Cholesterol	31 mg
Sodium	163 mg

* Percent Daily Values are based on a 2,000 calorie diet.

Thursday's Tenderloin

Ingredients

- 2 tbsp fresh rosemary
- 2 tbsp fresh thyme leaves
- 2 bay leaves
- 4 cloves garlic
- 1 large shallot, peeled and quartered
- 1 tbsp grated orange zest
- 1 tbsp coarse salt
- 1 tsp freshly ground black pepper
- 1/2 tsp ground nutmeg
- 1/4 tsp ground cloves
- 2 tbsp olive oil
- 2 (2 lb.) beef tenderloin roasts, trimmed

Directions

- In a food processor, add the rosemary, thyme, bay leaves, garlic, shallot, orange zest, salt, pepper, nutmeg and cloves and pulse till combined.
- While the motor is running slowly, add the oil and pulse till smooth.
- Coat the beef tenderloins with the pureed mixture evenly.
- In a large glass baking dish, place the beef tenderloins.

- With a piece of the foil, cover the baking dish and refrigerate for at least 6 hours.
- Set your oven to 400 degrees F and arrange a rack in a large roasting pan.
- Place the beef tenderloins over the rack in the roasting pan.
- Cook in the oven for about 35 minutes.
- Remove from oven and transfer onto a cutting board.
- With a piece of the foil, cover the tenderloins for about 10 minutes.
- Cut the tenderloins into slices and serve.

Amount per serving (8 total)

Timing Information:

Preparation	20 m
Cooking	35 m
Total Time	6 h 55 m

Nutritional Information:

Calories	683 kcal
Fat	55.8 g
Carbohydrates	2.3g
Protein	40.7 g
Cholesterol	161 mg
Sodium	831 mg

* Percent Daily Values are based on a 2,000 calorie diet.

Veggie Stir Fry

Ingredients

- 1 (12 oz.) box Barilla Gluten Free Penne
- 4 tbsp extra-virgin olive oil
- 1 shallot, minced
- 1 bunch asparagus, sliced diagonally
- 1 pint cherry tomatoes, halved
- 10 fresh basil leaves, torn
- 1/2 C. grated Parmesan cheese
- Salt and black pepper to taste

Directions

- In a large pan of the boiling water, prepare the pasta according to the package's directions.
- Drain well.
- Meanwhile, in a skillet, heat the olive oil on medium heat and sauté the shallots for about 2 minutes.
- Increase the heat to high and stir in the asparagus and tomatoes and sauté for about 2 minutes.
- Stir in the salt and pepper and remove from the heat.
- In a large bowl, add the pasta and vegetable mixture and toss to coat well.
- Add the cheese and basil and stir to combine.

- Serve immediately.

Amount per serving (5 total)

Timing Information:

Preparation	10 m
Cooking	15 m
Total Time	25 m

Nutritional Information:

Calories	413 kcal
Fat	14.6 g
Carbohydrates	61.7g
Protein	10.7 g
Cholesterol	7 mg
Sodium	162 mg

* Percent Daily Values are based on a 2,000 calorie diet.

Texas Fritters

Ingredients

- 2 3/4 C. sifted all-purpose flour
- 1 1/2 C. milk
- 6 tbsp shallots, chopped
- 2 tbsp chopped fresh parsley
- 2 tbsp baking powder
- 2 tsp salt
- 2 tsp ground black pepper
- 1 1/2 tsp dried thyme
- 6 C. grated carrots
- 2 C. vegetable oil for frying
- 1 C. béarnaise sauce

Directions

- In a large bowl, add the flour, milk, shallots, parsley, baking powder, salt, black pepper and thyme and mix till well combined.
- Gently fold in the carrots and refrigerate, covered for 3 hours.
- Heat vegetable oil in a deep fryer to 375 degrees F.
- With heaping tbsp, add the mixture into the hot oil in batches and fry for about 10-12 minutes.

- With a slotted spoon, transfer the fritters onto a paper towel lined plate to drain.
- Serve immediately alongside the Béarnaise sauce.

Amount per serving (20 total)

Timing Information:

Preparation	10 m
Cooking	40 m
Total Time	1 h 20 m

Nutritional Information:

Calories	140 kcal
Fat	6.1 g
Carbohydrates	18.4g
Protein	3 g
Cholesterol	25 mg
Sodium	455 mg

* Percent Daily Values are based on a 2,000 calorie diet.

Bangkok South Squid

Ingredients

- 6 shallots, finely chopped
- 4 cloves garlic, peeled and crushed
- 2 tbsp sambal belachan, or sriracha
- 2 tsp vegetable oil
- 1 tsp curry powder
- 1 tsp ground cumin
- 1 tsp fresh lime juice
- salt and pepper to taste
- 1 lb. squid, cleaned and sliced into rings
- 1 banana leaf

Directions

- In a non-reactive bowl, add the shallots, garlic, sambal belachan, vegetable oil, curry powder, cumin, lime juice, salt and pepper and mix till well combined.
- Gently, stir in the squid and refrigerate, covered for at least 2 hours.
- Set your outdoor grill for high heat and lightly, grease the grill grate.
- Lightly grease the banana leaf evenly.
- Place the squid in the center of the leaf.

- Carefully, wrap the leaf around the squid.
- Cook the banana wrap on the grill for about 10-15 minutes.

Amount per serving (2 total)

Timing Information:

Preparation	2 h 15 m
Cooking	15 m
Total Time	4 h 30 m

Nutritional Information:

Calories	409 kcal
Fat	8.2 g
Carbohydrates	43.9g
Protein	39.8 g
Cholesterol	529 mg
Sodium	251 mg

* Percent Daily Values are based on a 2,000 calorie diet.

Nanjing Dynasty Chicken

Ingredients

- 3 tbsp soy sauce
- 3 tbsp vegetable oil
- 2 tbsp sherry
- 2 shallots
- 6 cloves garlic
- 2 tbsp fresh ginger
- 2 tbsp Chinese five-spice powder
- 1 serrano pepper
- 2 tbsp brown sugar
- 1/2 tsp ground anise seed
- 1/2 tsp salt
- 2 lb. bone-in chicken parts

Directions

- In a food processor, add the soy sauce, oil, sherry, shallots, garlic, ginger, Chinese five-spice powder, Serrano pepper, brown sugar, anise and salt and pulse till smooth.
- Transfer the pureed mixture into a large bowl.
- Add the chicken parts and coat with the mixture generously.
- Refrigerate, covered for at least 1 hour.

- Set your grill for high heat and lightly, grease the grill grate.
- Remove the chicken parts from the bowl and discard the excess marinade.
- Cook the chicken parts on the grill for about 10 minutes per side.

Amount per serving (4 total)

Timing Information:

Preparation	15 m
Cooking	20 m
Total Time	1 h 35 m

Nutritional Information:

Calories	546 kcal
Fat	34.4 g
Carbohydrates	18.2g
Protein	40.1 g
Cholesterol	141 mg
Sodium	1146 mg

* Percent Daily Values are based on a 2,000 calorie diet.

Wild Salad

Ingredients

- 2 pears, cored and thinly sliced
- 1 C. diet lemon-lime soda
- 4 C. baby spinach leaves
- 1 shallot, finely chopped
- 1/2 C. crumbled feta cheese
- 1/2 C. toasted pine nuts
- 1/2 C. raspberry vinaigrette salad dressing

Directions

- In a bowl, mix together the pears and lemon-lime soda and keep aside till serving.
- Drain the pears well and discard the soda.
- In a large bowl, mix together the pears, baby spinach, shallot, feta cheese and pine nuts.
- Add the raspberry vinaigrette dressing and toss to coat well.

Amount per serving (4 total)

Timing Information:

Preparation	
Cooking	30 m
Total Time	30 m

Nutritional Information:

Calories	299 kcal
Fat	15.6 g
Carbohydrates	33.8g
Protein	10.1 g
Cholesterol	28 mg
Sodium	820 mg

* Percent Daily Values are based on a 2,000 calorie diet.

Award Winning Stuffing

Ingredients

- 2 C. hot water
- 1 oz. dried porcini mushrooms
- 1 3/4 lb. egg bread, crust trimmed
- 6 tbsp unsalted butter
- 4 C. coarsely chopped leeks
- 1 C. shallots, chopped
- 1 1/4 lb. Crimini mushrooms, sliced
- 1/2 lb. fresh sliced shiitake mushrooms
- 2 C. chopped celery
- 1 C. chopped fresh parsley
- 1 C. chopped toasted hazelnuts
- 3 tbsp chopped fresh thyme
- 2 tbsp chopped fresh sage
- 2 eggs
- 3/4 C. chicken stock
- salt to taste
- ground black pepper to taste
- 1 C. dried porcini mushrooms

Directions

- In a bowl, soak the porcini mushrooms in 2 C. of the hot water for about 30 minutes.
- Drain the mushrooms, reserving the soaking liquid.

- Squeeze the porcini mushrooms to dry and then chop roughly.
- Set your oven to 325 degrees F.
- Divide the bread cubes in 2 baking sheets evenly and cook in the oven for about 15 minutes.
- Remove from the oven and keep aside to cool completely.
- Transfer the toasted bread cubes into a very large bowl.
- In a heavy Dutch oven, melt the butter on medium-high heat and sauté the leeks, shallots, Crimini and shiitake mushrooms for about 15 minutes.
- Add the celery and porcini mushrooms and sauté for about 5 minutes.
- Transfer mixture into the bowl with the bread crumbs.
- Add the parsley, hazelnuts, thyme, sage, salt, pepper and beaten eggs and mix till ell combined.
- For the baking of whole stuffing, set your oven to 325 F and butter a 15x10x2-inch baking dish.
- In a bowl, mix together 3/4 C. of the reserved porcini soaking liquid and 3/4 C. of the broth.
- Add the broth mixture into the stuffing and stir till moisten.
- Transfer the stuffing mixture into the prepared baking dish evenly.
- With a buttered piece of the foil, cover the baking dish and cook in the oven for about 1 hour.
- Uncover and cook in the oven for about 15 minutes.
- For turkey, stuff the main cavity with the enough stuffing.

- In a bowl, mix together the broth and 1/2 C. of the reserved porcini soaking liquid.
- Add enough broth mixture to the remaining stuffing and mix till moisten.
- Transfer the moisten stuffing into a buttered baking dish.
- With a buttered piece of the foil, cover the baking dish and cook in the oven alongside the turkey for about 30 minutes.
- Uncover and cook in the oven for about 15 minutes.

Amount per serving (5 total)

Timing Information:

Preparation	30 m
Cooking	1 h
Total Time	1 h 40 m

Nutritional Information:

Calories	969 kcal
Fat	40.8 g
Carbohydrates	116.5g
Protein	37.5 g
Cholesterol	192 mg
Sodium	938 mg

* Percent Daily Values are based on a 2,000 calorie diet.

Omega-3 Patties

Ingredients

- 1/2 lb. salmon
- 1 red potato, peeled and chopped
- 1 shallot, minced
- 1 egg, beaten
- 1/4 C. Italian seasoned bread crumbs
- 1 tsp dried Italian seasoning
- salt and pepper to taste
- 1/2 C. cornflake crumbs
- 2 tbsp olive oil

Directions

- Set your oven to 350 degrees F before doing anything else and lightly, grease a small baking dish.
- Arrange the salmon into the prepared baking dish.
- Cover the baking dish and cook in the oven for about 20 minutes.
- In a small pan of the water, add the potatoes and bring to a boil.
- Cook for about 15 minutes.
- Drain the potatoes and then mash them.

- In a bowl, add the salmon, potato, shallot, egg, bread crumbs, Italian seasoning, salt and pepper and mix till well combined.
- In a shallow bowl, place the cornflake crumbs.
- Make about 1-inch balls from the salmon mixture.
- Coat the balls with the cornflakes crumb mixture evenly and then gently, press each ball into a patty.
- In a medium pan, heat the olive oil on medium heat and fry the patties for about 3-5 minutes per side.

Amount per serving (6 total)

Timing Information:

Preparation	15 m
Cooking	45 m
Total Time	1 h

Nutritional Information:

Calories	194 kcal
Fat	9.3 g
Carbohydrates	18.2g
Protein	9.5 g
Cholesterol	50 mg
Sodium	354 mg

* Percent Daily Values are based on a 2,000 calorie diet.

Lamb Burgers Classical

Ingredients

- 1/2 C. mayonnaise
- 1 tsp minced garlic
- 2 lb. ground lamb
- 1/4 C. breadcrumbs
- 1 C. trimmed, diced fennel bulb
- 3 tbsp shallots, minced
- 1 tsp dried oregano
- 1/2 tsp salt
- ground black pepper to taste
- 1 tbsp olive oil
- 8 hamburger buns

Directions

- In a small bowl, mix together the mayonnaise and minced garlic and refrigerate, covered for at least 1 hour.
- Set your grill for high heat and grease the grill grate with 1 tsp of the olive oil.
- In a bowl, add the lamb, breadcrumbs, fennel, shallot, oregano, and salt and mix till well combined.
- Make about 3/4-inch-thick patties from the mixture.
- Sprinkle each patty with the black pepper.

- Cook the patties on the grill for about 3-5 minutes per side.
- Place the patties over the buns with the garlic mayonnaise and serve.

Amount per serving (8 total)

Timing Information:

Preparation	25 m
Cooking	10 m
Total Time	1 h 35 m

Nutritional Information:

Calories	479 kcal
Fat	30.4 g
Carbohydrates	26.2g
Protein	23.9 g
Cholesterol	81 mg
Sodium	559 mg

* Percent Daily Values are based on a 2,000 calorie diet.

New England Crab Lunch

Ingredients

- 1 C. dry sherry
- 1 tbsp finely chopped shallots
- 1 green bell pepper, finely chopped
- 6 fresh mushrooms, thinly sliced
- 1 pimento, chopped
- 1/2 C. heavy cream
- 1 egg yolk
- 1 tsp dry mustard
- 1 lb. cooked crabmeat, flaked
- 1 C. mayonnaise
- 1/2 C. Gruyeres cheese, shredded

Directions

- Set your oven to 400 degrees F before doing anything else and lightly, grease 6 small baking dishes.
- In a medium pan, add the sherry on medium heat and bring to a boil.
- Stir in the shallots, green bell pepper, mushrooms and pimento and cook till only a little amount of liquid remains, stirring occasionally.

- In a small pan, add the heavy cream and egg yolk on low heat and cook for about 3 minutes, beating continuously.
- Transfer the cream mixture into the shallot mixture.
- Add the dry mustard and stir to combine.
- Remove from the heat and stir in the crab.
- Keep aside to cool.
- Add the mayonnaise and stir to combine.
- Transfer the mixture into the prepared baking dishes evenly and sprinkle with the Gruyeres cheese.
- Cook in the oven for about 10 minutes.

Amount per serving (6 total)

Timing Information:

Preparation	20 m
Cooking	25 m
Total Time	1 h

Nutritional Information:

Calories	513 kcal
Fat	41.3 g
Carbohydrates	11.2g
Protein	21.8 g
Cholesterol	143 mg
Sodium	776 mg

* Percent Daily Values are based on a 2,000 calorie diet.

PILAF POSSIBILITIES

Ingredients

- 1 tbsp olive oil
- 1 shallot, minced
- 2 cloves garlic, minced
- 1 medium red bell pepper, diced
- 1 medium yellow bell pepper, diced
- 1 C. uncooked quinoa, rinsed
- 2 C. Swanson(R) Certified Organic Vegetable Broth
- 2 tbsp chopped fresh parsley

Directions

- In a 2-quart pan heat the oil on medium-high heat and sauté the shallot and garlic for about 2 minutes.
- Add the peppers and quinoa and cook for about 2 minutes, stirring occasionally.
- Stir in the broth and bring to a boil.
- Reduce the heat to low and cook, covered for about 20 minutes.
- Stir in the parsley and serve.

Amount per serving (4 total)

Timing Information:

Preparation	
Cooking	20 m
Total Time	50 m

Nutritional Information:

Calories	223 kcal
Fat	6.1 g
Carbohydrates	35.2g
Protein	7.1 g
Cholesterol	0 mg
Sodium	272 mg

* Percent Daily Values are based on a 2,000 calorie diet.

Mediterranean Fish

Ingredients

- 1/4 C. canola oil for pan-frying
- 4 (7 oz.) halibut fillets
- Kosher salt and fresh cracked pepper to taste
- 1/4 C. all-purpose flour for dredging

For the sauce:

- 2 tbsp unsalted butter
- 2 shallots, minced
- 2 oz. thickly sliced Spanish serrano ham, cut into 1/4-inch dice, optional
- 1/4 C. golden raisins, soaked in hot water to soften
- 2 tbsp capers, rinsed and patted dry
- 1/4 C. pine nuts, lightly toasted
- 1/3 C. Calvados (apple brandy)
- 1/2 C. chicken stock
- 1/2 C. cold unsalted butter, cut into pieces
- 1 tbsp minced fresh parsley
- 2 tsp minced fresh thyme
- Kosher salt to taste

Directions

- Set your oven to 450 degrees F before doing anything else.
- Season the halibut fillets with the salt and pepper.

- Coat the halibut fillets with the flour and shake off the excess.
- In a large, oven proof skillet, heat the canola oil on high heat and sear the halibut steaks for about 1 minute per side.
- Drain the excess oil from the skillet.
- Transfer the skillet into the oven, and cook for about 7-8 minutes.
- Remove the halibut steaks from skillet and place into a bowl.
- With a piece of the foil, over the steaks to keep them warm.
- In a pan, melt 2 tbsp of the butter on medium heat and sauté the shallots for about 1 minute.
- Add the ham, drained raisins, capers and pine nuts and sauté for about 1 minute.
- Add the Calvados and cook till the mixture reduces by half.
- Add the chicken stock and increase the heat to high.
- Boil till 1/4 of the stock is evaporated.
- Remove the pan from the heat and immediately add 1/2 C. of the butter and beat till melts completely.
- Add the parsley, thyme and salt and stir to combine.
- Divide the halibut onto serving plates and serve immediately with a topping of the sauce.

Amount per serving (4 total)

Timing Information:

Preparation	15 m
Cooking	20 m
Total Time	35 m

Nutritional Information:

Calories	777 kcal
Fat	56.4 g
Carbohydrates	20.1g
Protein	48.8 g
Cholesterol	153 mg
Sodium	732 mg

* Percent Daily Values are based on a 2,000 calorie diet.

CENTRAL AMERICAN PASTA

Ingredients

- 1 (8 oz.) package cavatappi pasta
- 1 tsp olive oil
- 1 tsp butter
- 1 shallot, chopped
- 2 cloves garlic, diced
- 1 dried habanero pepper, chopped
- 2 C. heavy cream
- 1 large tomato, diced
- 2 tbsp all-purpose flour
- 1 tsp black pepper
- 1 C. grated Parmesan cheese

Directions

- In a large pan of lightly salted boiling water, cook the egg noodles for about 5 minutes.
- Drain well and keep aside.
- In a skillet, melt the butter and olive oil on medium heat and sauté the shallots, garlic and habanero pepper till golden browned.
- Add the cream and bring to a simmer.

- Stir in the tomato, flour and black pepper and simmer for about 5-8 minutes.
- Stir in the Parmesan cheese and remove from the heat.
- Keep aside to cool for a few minutes.
- Place the sauce over the pasta and serve.

Amount per serving (4 total)

Timing Information:

Preparation	10 m
Cooking	15 m
Total Time	25 m

Nutritional Information:

Calories	755 kcal
Fat	52.9 g
Carbohydrates	53.6g
Protein	19 g
Cholesterol	183 mg
Sodium	365 mg

* Percent Daily Values are based on a 2,000 calorie diet.

Augusta Pudding

Ingredients

- 2 tbsp butter
- 1/2 C. shallots, minced
- 1/4 C. fresh Poblano chili pepper, seeded and chopped
- 12 oz. frozen corn kernels, thawed
- 1 3/4 C. half-and-half cream
- 6 eggs
- 3 tbsp all-purpose flour
- 1 1/2 tsp salt
- 1 tsp white sugar
- 1/4 tsp ground nutmeg
- 1/4 tsp ground white pepper
- 1 1/2 C. cooked crabmeat
- 4 tbsp grated Parmesan cheese

Directions

- Set your oven to 350 degrees F before doing anything else and lightly, grease 8 (3/4 C.) soufflé dishes.
- In a heavy skillet, melt the butter on medium heat and sauté the shallots and Poblano pepper for about 3 minutes.
- In a food processor, add the corn and pulse till pureed.

- Add half-and-half, eggs, flour, salt, sugar, nutmeg and white pepper and pulse till smooth.
- Transfer the pureed mixture into large bowl.
- Add the crab meat and Poblano chili mixture and stir to combine.
- Divide the mixture into the prepared soufflé dishes evenly and Sprinkle with cheese.
- In a large roasting pan, arrange the soufflé dishes and add enough hot water in the pan to come halfway up sides.
- Cook in the oven for about 50 minutes or till a toothpick inserted in the center comes out clean.

Amount per serving (8 total)

Timing Information:

Preparation	30 m
Cooking	50 m
Total Time	1 h 20 m

Nutritional Information:

Calories	245 kcal
Fat	14.1 g
Carbohydrates	16.4g
Protein	14.8 g
Cholesterol	188 mg
Sodium	668 mg

* Percent Daily Values are based on a 2,000 calorie diet.

Avenida Salsa

Ingredients

- 2 lb. tomatillos, husked and cut in half
- 3 green tomatoes, chopped
- 1/2 C. olive oil
- 2 mild chili peppers, chopped
- 1 shallot, chopped
- 5 sprigs cilantro, chopped
- 1/3 C. distilled white vinegar
- 1/4 C. garlic powder to taste
- 1 tsp salt

Directions

- In a large pan, add the tomatillos, tomatoes, oil, chili pepper, shallots, cilantro, vinegar, garlic powder and salt on medium-high heat and bring to a boil.
- Reduce the heat to medium-low and simmer for about 15-20 minutes.
- In a blender, add the mixture and pulse till smooth.
- Remove from the heat and transfer into a bowl.
- Refrigerate to chill before serving.

Amount per serving (20 total)

Timing Information:

Preparation	15 m
Cooking	15 m
Total Time	30 m

Nutritional Information:

Calories	76 kcal
Fat	5.9 g
Carbohydrates	5.7g
Protein	1.1 g
Cholesterol	0 mg
Sodium	121 mg

* Percent Daily Values are based on a 2,000 calorie diet.

Scallop Platter

Ingredients

- 1 shallot, sliced crosswise
- 1 tsp olive oil
- 1 pinch salt
- 1/4 C. finely chopped pineapple
- 1 tbsp freshly grated ginger
- 1 tbsp lemon grass, finely chopped
- 1 tsp cilantro, finely chopped
- 1 tsp honey
- 1 tsp apple cider vinegar
- 1/2 tsp sesame seeds
- 1/8 tsp red pepper flakes
- 4 tsp extra-virgin olive oil
- salt, to taste
- 1/2 lb. French style green beans, trimmed
- 2 tbsp safflower oil
- 4 large sea scallops

Directions

- In a skillet, heat 1 tsp of the olive oil on medium heat and sauté the shallot and 1 pinch of the salt for about 5 minutes.
- Transfer the shallot into a large bowl.
- Add the pineapple, ginger, lemon grass, cilantro, honey, vinegar, sesame seeds, red pepper flakes, extra virgin olive oil and salt and mix well.
- Arrange a steamer basket into a pan and fill with water to just below the bottom of the steamer basket.
- Bring the water to a boil over high heat and steam the green beans, covered for about 3-6 minutes.
- Drain and immediately immerse in the bowl of ice water for several minutes to stop the cooking process.
- After cooling, drain the green beans well and keep aside.
- With the paper towels, dry the scallop completely.
- In a large skillet, heat the safflower oil on high heat and sear the scallops for about 1 minute, without moving them.
- Flip the scallop and cook for about 90 seconds.
- Turn off the heat and immediately, transfer the scallops into a bowl.
- Immediately, add the green beans into the hot skillet and toss for about 1 minute.
- Divide the green beans into the serving plates evenly.
- Place the scallops over the green beans and serve with a topping of the pineapple salsa.

Amount per serving (2 total)

Timing Information:

Preparation	25 m
Cooking	20 m
Total Time	45 m

Nutritional Information:

Calories	368 kcal
Fat	26.5 g
Carbohydrates	16.7g
Protein	15.6 g
Cholesterol	26 mg
Sodium	500 mg

* Percent Daily Values are based on a 2,000 calorie diet.

Broccoli Soup

Ingredients

- 2 tbsp extra-virgin olive oil
- 1 small carrot, finely chopped
- 1 shallot, finely chopped
- 1/2 rib celery, finely chopped
- 3 1/2 oz. Romanesco broccoli, tough parts discarded, chopped
- 2 small potatoes, peeled and chopped
- 4 C. hot water
- salt and ground black pepper to taste

Directions

- In a pan, heat the olive oil on medium-low heat and sauté the carrot, shallot and celery for about 2-3 minutes.
- Add the Romanesco broccoli, potatoes, hot water, salt and pepper and cook, covered for about 40 minutes.
- With an immersion blender, blend the soup till smooth.
- Serve hot.

Amount per serving (2 total)

Timing Information:

Preparation	25 m
Cooking	42 m
Total Time	1 h 7 m

Nutritional Information:

Calories	295 kcal
Fat	13.8 g
Carbohydrates	39.4g
Protein	5.4 g
Cholesterol	0 mg
Sodium	150 mg

* Percent Daily Values are based on a 2,000 calorie diet.

How to Stuffed Mushrooms

Ingredients

- 36 Crimini mushrooms, stems removed
- 1/2 C. olive oil
- 2 1/2 C. chopped yellow onion
- 1/3 C. minced shallot
- 6 cloves garlic, minced
- 3 tbsp chopped Italian flat leaf parsley
- 3/4 C. chopped fresh chives
- 3 fluid oz. lemon juice
- 2 C. fresh bread crumbs
- 5 oz. shredded Gruyere cheese

Directions

- In a large pan of lightly salted boiling water, cook the mushrooms for about 3 minutes.
- Drain well and keep aside to cool.
- In a large skillet, heat the olive oil on medium heat and cook the onion, shallot, garlic, parsley, and chives, covered for a few minutes to release the aromas.
- Remove from the heat and immediately, stir in the breadcrumbs and lemon juice.
- Set the broiler of your oven.

- Scoop out the mushroom caps and stuff with the shallot mixture.
- Arrange the mushroom caps onto a baking sheet and top with the shredded cheese.
- Cook under the broiler for about 3-5 minutes.
- These stuffed mushroom caps will be great if served hot.

Amount per serving (12 total)

Timing Information:

Preparation	15 m
Cooking	10 m
Total Time	25 m

Nutritional Information:

Calories	188 kcal
Fat	13.1 g
Carbohydrates	10.8g
Protein	7.2 g
Cholesterol	13 mg
Sodium	115 mg

* Percent Daily Values are based on a 2,000 calorie diet.

ANNIVERSARY NIGHT MARSALA

Ingredients

- 2 tbsp olive oil
- 1 lb. veal medallions
- 1 C. all-purpose flour
- salt and pepper to taste
- 1 large shallot, minced
- 1 lb. fresh mushrooms, sliced
- 1 C. dry Marsala
- 1 clove garlic, minced
- 2 C. low-chicken broth
- 1 C. low-beef broth
- 2 tbsp unsalted butter

Directions

- Set your oven to 250 degrees F before doing anything else and line a baking dish with a piece of the foil.
- Coat the veal medallions with the flour slightly and season with the salt and pepper.
- In a skillet, heat 1 tbsp of the olive oil on medium-high heat and cook the veal medallions for about 5 minutes.
- With a slotted spoon, transfer veal medallions into the prepared baking dish.

- Place the baking dish in the preheated oven to keep warm before serving.
- In the same skillet, heat the remaining olive oil on medium-low heat and sauté the shallot and mushrooms till tender, scraping up any browned bits from the bottom and sides of the skillet.
- Now, increase the heat to medium-high and stir in the Marsala and garlic.
- Cook till the mixture becomes thick, stirring continuously.
- Stir in the chicken broth and beef broth and cook till the mixture reduces to about 1/4 C, stirring continuously.
- Remove from the heat and immediately, add the butter and bet till melted.
- Serve the veal with a topping of the Marsala mixture.

Amount per serving (4 total)

Timing Information:

Preparation	15 m
Cooking	20 m
Total Time	35 m

Nutritional Information:

Calories	491 kcal
Fat	18.3 g
Carbohydrates	43.9g
Protein	23.6 g
Cholesterol	73 mg
Sodium	314 mg

* Percent Daily Values are based on a 2,000 calorie diet.

Mississippi Corn

Ingredients

- 3 tbsp butter
- 1/4 C. shallots, minced
- 1 pinch sugar
- 2 C. frozen corn kernels
- 2 tbsp water
- 1/2 C. whipping cream
- 1 pinch ground nutmeg
- salt to taste

Directions

- In a large skillet, melt the butter on medium heat and sauté the shallots and sugar for about 2-3 minutes.
- Stir in the corn and water and cook for about 5 minutes.
- Slowly, add the cream, stirring continuously.
- Cook for about 8 minutes.
- Stir in the nutmeg, salt and pepper and remove from the heat.

Amount per serving (4 total)

Timing Information:

Preparation	10 m
Cooking	15 m
Total Time	25 m

Nutritional Information:

Calories	277 kcal
Fat	20.8 g
Carbohydrates	23.5g
Protein	3.7 g
Cholesterol	64 mg
Sodium	365 mg

* Percent Daily Values are based on a 2,000 calorie diet.

How to Make Egg Salad

Ingredients

- 8 large eggs
- 1/2 C. sour cream
- 3 tbsp finely chopped shallots
- 1 1/2 tbsp finely chopped fresh tarragon
- 2 tsp white wine vinegar
- 1/4 tsp salt
- 1/4 tsp black pepper
- 8 slices whole grain bread
- baby spinach leaves (optional)
- sliced tomatoes (optional)

Directions

- In a 2-quart heavy pan of water, add the eggs and bring to a rolling boil, partially covered.
- Reduce the heat to low and cook, covered for about 30 seconds.
- Remove from the heat and keep aside, covered for about 15 minutes.
- With a slotted spoon, transfer the eggs into a bowl of chilled water and keep aside for about 5 minutes.
- Peel the eggs and chop them finely.

- In a bowl, add the eggs and remaining salad ingredients and with a fork, mix well.
- Spread the egg salad over the bread slices evenly.
- Serve with a topping of your favorite garnishing.

Servings per Recipe: 4

Timing Information:

| Preparation | 10 mins |
| Total Time | 20 mins |

Nutritional Information:

Calories	347.8
Fat	17.2g
Cholesterol	386.9mg
Sodium	576.7mg
Carbohydrates	26.9g
Protein	21.0g

* Percent Daily Values are based on a 2,000 calorie diet.

THANKS FOR READING! JOIN THE CLUB AND KEEP ON COOKING WITH 6 MORE COOKBOOKS....

http://bit.ly/1TdrStv

To grab the box sets simply follow the link mentioned above, or tap one of book covers.

This will take you to a page where you can simply enter your email address and a PDF version of the box sets will be emailed to you.

Hope you are ready for some serious cooking!

http://bit.ly/1TdrStv

COME ON...
LET'S BE FRIENDS :)

We adore our readers and love connecting with them socially.

Like BookSumo on Facebook and let's get social!

Facebook

And also check out the BookSumo Cooking Blog.

Food Lover Blog

Printed in Great Britain
by Amazon